For Everyone

About
Lessons & Love & Heartbreak

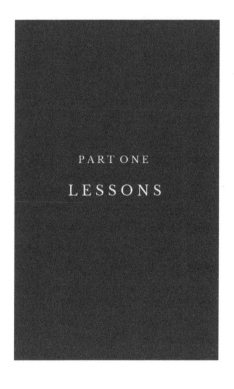

PART ONE

LESSONS

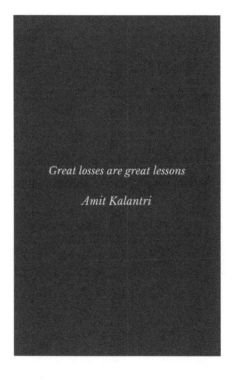

Great losses are great lessons

Amit Kalantri

MOTHER'S WORDS

*To express is to feel and to feel is to express, those
are the words my mother stressed*

*The ability to feel is more powerful than the
ability to see, she said*

*Because only when you feel, can you see and once
you can see, are you able to feel*

This is the key to life, she sensed

*At the time, all this was too much for me to digest
Too many layers of unanswered inquest
Too little time to ponder over her silly zest
Too young to understand my ignorant protest*

*But gone now are the days of my mother's quest
She lay's buried underneath the gravel, rest
Oh! I wish I tried harder to invest
A bit more time and thought into her request*

*I now lay in this nest
Waiting to pass on to the next
Time really does flies, I guess
Only yesterday was I a guest
And I am now fleeing like rest*

MOTHER'S WORDS

If I am truthful, I am terrified underneath my chest

For what the coming life or death has, a test?

I guess, my message to you is to feel and then to express

To Feel and then to see, the wonderful life you enjoy at ease

Don't suffer the painfulness of my test

Don't follow the footsteps of my painful quest

An Ignorance of a truthful pretest

Only to find out you have hours to digest an 80 year life with a swift zest

So feel, see, love, and express

PUNISHMENT

On a cold winter night, an old man sat under a park tree

All alone, he rested with misery

Then by the passing of a few moments, a strange being approached and sat down next to him in company

It asked him why on earth he was in a park, alone covered in misery?

The old man shivering faster than an eating squirrel replied, "why don't you just let me be!

Why don't you just get on with your life and leave me underneath this tree?"

The being smiling replied, I'm afraid that can't be the case until you answer me

So answer me, old man, I am sitting with you underneath this tree

PUNISHMENT

Stung, the old man's sagging mask spoke of
confusion while his eyes glorified the being's
bravery

Never in his life has another soul asked of him
anything so dearly

That the thought of someone else even caring to
ask such a selfless question out of curiosity or
humility, made him want to shed tears like a
baby

The old man Stuttering spoke finally
He said, in his 92 years living no one spoke wi
such modesty

That the being was the first to care of him,
genuinely

And of his reason as to why he had been initial
sitting under a tree in misery

Because in his opinion, people say they care bu
deep within they only care of themselves truly

PUNISHMENT

*And all his life he has been touched by nothing
but calamity*

*Imprisoned with immorality
Treated with absolutely no dignity
Incarcerated with loneliness, depression, illness,
and anxiety*

*Destitute to a life of mute isolation by the
starvation of constant fatality*

Now, he hangs on by a thin rope, his sanity

*Crying the being replied, you have spoken the
truth
I have been watching you all your life, my name
is Ruth
I am an angel, and I come from the 4th haven,
Lueth*

*I have been assigned to protect you from the sun
and expose you to the darkness of the moon*

*To prevent the human light within you to bloom
To be and see not a life of youthfulness until
your tomb*

PUNISHMENT

This may be hard to accept and consume, but this has been my assignment sent down from the tooth

A punishment, no rather a test for you, from the highest being, I think you know who.

The old man confused, finally asked, "so why am I being punished?"

And the angel relied because you have been chosen to pay for humanity's evil dooms

GREATNESS OF PAIN

Pain is the cause of pleasure unmet
Unlike pleasure, pain is a reminder of what we
could have net

But in our shallow, battered self, pain repeats
our debt
In our mind, we are the victim, and pain is the
threat

But what is pleasure without pain?
What is grass without rain?
What is work without gain?
What is blood without a vain?
Worthless!

You see without pain, we can not experience
pleasure the same

Without pain, there is nothing to blame, and to
aim, so that we can then one day claim, a better
life because of the lessons we learned from our
pain

Pain is not the enemy of progress, nor is it the
nemesis of happiness

GREATNESS OF PAIN

It is only there so that we may realize the importance of our sloppiness and our mindlessness so that we may correct our effortlessness

In order to grow and gain the pleasure that our pain helped us acquire

SUNSHINE

The sun is always shining brother said to me
It's just the clouds that get in the way don't you
see.
You see, the sun is always shinning but
sometimes the clouds don't agree

With the fairness of the sun's playtime with you
and me
So they bicker and batter, and come up with a
plan to play with you and me
Eventually, each agree that they will have ample
time to aid you and me

That on certain days, the clouds will float in the
horizon with a breeze, providing a cooling air
for us to breath

While on some days they will hold still
Raining down a refreshing shower as they help
mama and papa grow their trees and provide
nourishment for the animals to drink and eat

While on some days the sun will have its turn to
play with you and me

SUNSHINE

t will light our whole world bright as it can be
Providing us a healthy dose of vitamin D

So that we can grow like that tall strong tree
and help mama and papa when they grow like
that weak ancient bee

PROTECTOR

What does protection even mean?
Well, by definition, it's someone or something
that defends someone or something

But that doesn't hold up because there's still
something missing

Like tall grass out in the open, there is
something hissing

Or the example of an invisible man where the
only thing visible is the arch of his pissing

Alright! I think you get the point, so i'll stop
twisting

According to my own definition, the meaning of
protection is something along the lines of
kissing

Wait. Let me explain myself first before you get
the wrong impression

Protection is like kissing because both involve
selection

PROTECTOR

*Only when a being chooses you among another
for the sole purpose of your stability, are you
then able to experience true protection*

*This involves an element of emotional bond; One
must feel towards you, a magnetic connection*

*Almost as if losing you because of one's error as
your life hangs in the balance, will cause them
great personal destruction*

*Understand: Protection is defense and defense is
support and support is provision and provision
is preparation pointing to protection*

*Protection is not something that must be
obtained through painful affliction
Nor does it need to be obtained by one's begging*

*It is simply the combination of emotional
connection and disciplined suitable action*

PROTECTOR

This, I feel, is the true worthy
definition of a protector.
So be a protector and
protect those whome
you love!

TRIANGLE

Education doesn't equal knowledge, nor does knowledge equal wisdom

Each element is within it's own element
You can learn something for years, yet lack sufficient education in order to display a solid foundation of knowledge
This then prevents you from gaining any real wisdom, and the opposite is true

You can have a solid education yet lack knowledge
You can have knowledge yet lack wisdom
You can have wisdom but lack education

Education doesn't equal knowledge, and knowledge doesn't equal wisdom

21

MIND

Free the mind
Let it be
Let it sore until it can no more

Give it permission to think
Give it permission to bleed

To see where the blood or seed of its thoughts
lead

After all, isn't that what it's made to do

Isn't the mind meant to provide

A solution as well as a problem

As to see what it secretly harbors or finds
inevitably awesome

I believe this to be true

So, let your mind bloom

REBELS

To the wild ones who play endlessly
with wilderness
Who are quite, shy, and timid
or maniacs when alone
Who cannot for the life of them be fitted,
squired, and shut tightly into a restricting,
inflexible, box of conformity
Who when told what to do, what to feel, and
how to act, create hurricanes of chaos
shaking even the bravest among us to our core
Who when something is unaligned with their
understanding of things, question every
normalizing chain of thought
Who stand for the poor, the ill, and restless

These are the ones
who have been touched
by god

BIRTH DAY

A birth day is a reminder of a coming day
when you will crumble like sand and
your bones weak,
will fall apart like clay
perishing
into thin air,
as your ashes
fly
away

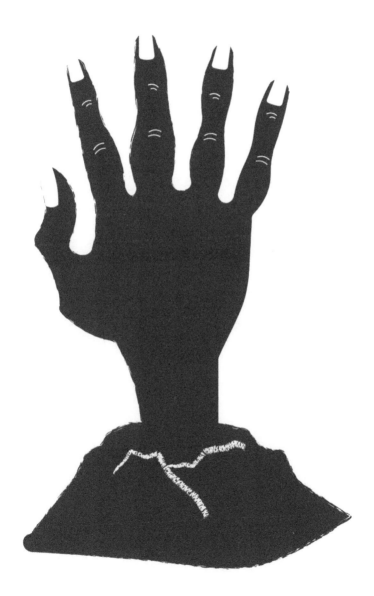

SOUL

The *skin on your bones*

The hair on your skin

The clothes on your back

The shoes on your feet

ll mean nothing without the uniqueness of your soul

TIME

Tick tock, that clock flocks

By the movement of a longhand, it jogs

By the movement of a shorthand, it walks

Chasing each other, they tick and tock

Tocking until it hits a new o'clock

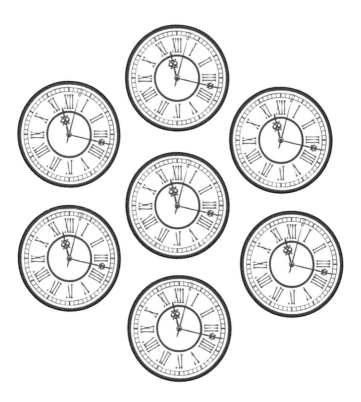

DESTINY

*Destined are you the one who works towards a
better life
Blessed should you and blessed will you be until
another life
For this world is a pit stop and the next is your
final afterlife*

SOULMATES

Sleep but do not sleep for too long

*For sleep is the soulmate of death and
death is the soulmate of sleep*

*They are bound to meet
binding their love,
your death*

HEROES

*There are some beautiful souls
among us on this planet*

Unsung

*Who are aiding the human
story towards a happily ever
after*

DANCE

We should dance more
It teaches us to let go and
move with a rhythm of life

LIFE & DEATH

Birth equals life and life equals death
Inseparable are they like the nose that allows you
to draw breath

THOUGHTS

*Our life is a reflection of our thoughts,
and our eyes are it's projector*

POORLY RICH MAN

A poor man once told me he was the
richest man in the world

Not because he had moutains of money
but rather he had happiness in his heart

Something no one could ever take away
from him

MASTERPIECE

We are all artists creating the masterpiece of our lives through our daily experiences

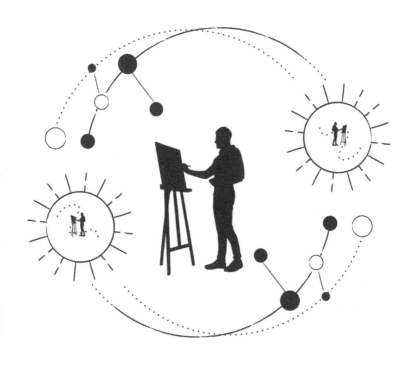

PEOPLE

We respect the elders because they are our past
The youth becuase they are our present
And the children becasue they are our future

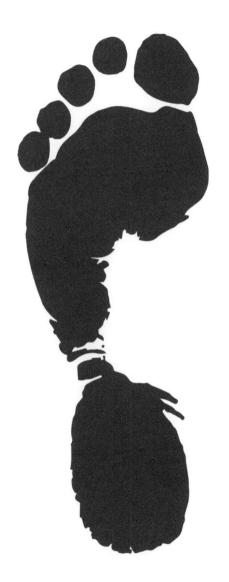

WATER

She is water
A giver of life
A taker of life

VICE VERSA

*What is broken has the
capability to heal
Just as what is fixed has the
ability to be broken*

CAGED BIRD

Sometimes you have to cut the strings
that hold you back by your feet and fly
high into the air so that you can see,
you were only a bird trapped in a cage

RIPE

When the time is ripe you must put
your foot down and shake the earth
Letting all who stand in your way
know your worth

LOVE

In the end love always wins
and hate always hates

HEALING

Hope is my only healer
My comforter and protector
Providing me warmth against this
barbarous place we all call home,
earth

WIND DREAMER

*May the wind be the vessel in which
you reach your farthest dreams*

PLAYGROUND

*The world is a big playground
so what are you waiting for,
go play around*

UNIVERSE

The universe is universal
What goes around comes around, eventually

BREATH

The essence of life is with the breath
because life begins with a single breath
and ends with a single breath

DROWNING PAIN

Do not drown by the pain of your pain rather
drown the pain
Drown the pain that causes you pain and
drown the thoughts that cause you pain
Drown the feelings that cause you pain and
drown the situations that cause you pain
Drowning them until they no longer feel what
it's like to drown you in pain

SUNNY

The sun is always shining it's just the
clouds that get in the way and blind us
in the darkness

WILDER

Be wild and free
for youth lasts so long

ACHIEVER

*A dreamer is only an achiever running
towards a dream unachieved*

UNIQUENESS

*No one else can play the main character
within the movie of your life because
only you have that talent*

IMAGINE

*I believe education is the
product of imagination*

GREEDY JEALOUSY

Avoid the jealous and greedy
for poison bleeds in their hearts

SELF CRITIC

In the darkness of your privacy
When no one is watching except the critical critic,
I want you to know you are still beautiful

TIME

The difference between family and
friends is not by blood but time
for time can turn enemies into friends
friends into enemies, family into friends
and friends into family

BEGIN

There is no end without a beginning
So just begin and you'll find your end

DEEDS

I believe one good deed can erase many wrong deeds and one bad deed has the power to erase many good deeds

LIFE & DEATH

Understand death and you overcome
life
Understand life and you overcome
death

CRYING SKY

The sky cries just like you and i
But it cries for all of us, you and i

RAINING SKY

*Because without the sky there would be no rain
and without rain there would be no life*

SCALES

The scales are unbalanced
and
There is nothing that can balance
love

PRICE

Everything has a price
it's just up to you to decide
how much you want to sacrifice

SOMEDAY

Someday you'll make an impression on someone you barely know and it will be the last you ever see of them

ALONE

There's an art to being alone
Alone in your own loneliness
Without ever feeling lonely

LIFE

How can you be lifeless
when you give life

MARVELOUS

See beauty in your eyes, not in the eyes of society
Give light to the presence of whatever you feel is
beautiful and allow the growth of what is not yet
beautiful to manifest into perfection

Accept the singularity of your life so that it may
shine a spotlight on the darkness of another,
helping it understand it's own beauty in a world
full of Consummation
A world glorifying the eminence of a few
Only to broadcast them in full view
And convince you, that there is no other, who?

Understand your own perfection and understand
your own glory

That you, among the millions who live on this
earth, is a chosen new

That there will never be another you
To walk on this earth ever again when your time
is due
So I urge you to seek your own validation
To submit to your own completion
To rise in your own amplification
And to understand your own navigation

PART TWO

LOVE

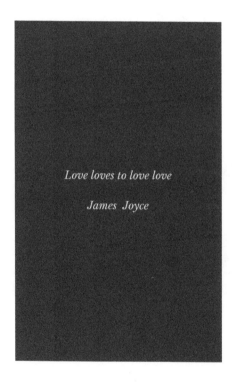

Love loves to love love

James Joyce

KNOWN WOMEN

*Cold and tired I stand here frozen looking deep
into the eyes of this women*

*Eyes I have only met seconds but feel I've always
known*

*Shivering, I straighten up my smile, fix my
posture, and clear my throat, ready to show her
a gentleman*

*Below, my knees buckle in weakness and
thumping in my heart drums in celebration,
feelings I have never known*

*Beauty and perfection outline the configuration
of this matron — a goddess among the presence
of queens, unknown*

*I can feel the heated speed of my mind gear up to
speak of my fascination*

*Trying to formulate my thoughts, order my
words, and clear passage for this information
I swallow my thirst, open my mouth, dripping in
fear this is uncommon*

KNOWN WOMEN

*A whisper let's out, shallow than the loudest
bird, unheard*

I try again, maybe this time I'll be heard

*"Hey honey! " a strang man interrupts, grabbing
her steadily*

"We've gotta go!" he says, calmly

Shocked by the reality, I look away humbly

Bothered by this melody, I can feel the agony

*Feeling like my heart was in the hands of
harmony, then crushed by this complexity*

KNOWN WOMEN

*Hypnotized, she now stares at me, as he drags
her away from me*

*Oh, I just had an epiphany
I can't believe it, that man is running away with
my soul mate, crushed by this honesty.*

*Leaves turn, seasons return, lessons yearn, I
think I might have run into her turn*

*Soaking up the Venice air and toasting in the
sun, sitting there is my Madison*

*Speechless my sunglasses rise, and my eyes blink
twice
I scan her to match the blueprint of her former
self, and it's precise*

*She look's alone, why don't I aid, I think
Decided, I sip my tropical watermelon on last
time, put it aside, and head over to link*

*We now sit at the wooden table, gazing fully at
each other as if the keys of our souls have
unlocked the chambers within*

KNOWN WOMEN

Talking and talking some more, we talked until the sun swapped with the moon

An ora of simplicity and ease carried the conversation, while a sense within birthed a bloom

My trip turned into our trip, and a trip turned into a journey

Our journey continued, leading us onto thrilling adventures, dinners, dances, and unforgettable moments

However, nothing will top that night Cold and happy I lowed my knee into the thick Smush of snow, looking deep into the eyes of this women

Eyes I have met and feel I'll always know!

PARIS

She said I love Paris
and i've loved Paris ever since

SELFISH

*I'm doing this for us because
your too selfish to be selfless*

WINKING STAR

I can see you way up there
among the stars, winking at me

HOME

I feel as if at times you have a magical rope that pulls me back from my lingering mind somewhere in space and you bring me back to my home, you

CONFUSED LOVE

Through all the chaos and confusion that
surrounds us, i want you to know
I love you and cherish you more each day

EYES

*It's her eyes that make her
So dangerous*

CONTAGIOUS

Your smile is infectious
Your laugh, contagious
Your thoughts are precious
And your touch makes me breathless

SMILE

The sky is happy, its blue
The sun is shinning, it's yellow
Only thing missing is your smile, silly

HURRICANE VEINS

The thought of losing you
boils a hurricane through
my veins

U S

Together we can be
anything you want
us to be

GLUE

I love you like glue
All I want is to be attached to you
To never let you go, because who knows what
will happen if I do

LOVE

Love is like a panther that waits for you in the shadows, unexpected Jumping onto you at you weakest as it clings it's claws deep into your beating heart until you submit and fall within the ocean of love

STAR WATCHING

Maybe we'll meet on the moon and watch the stars someday

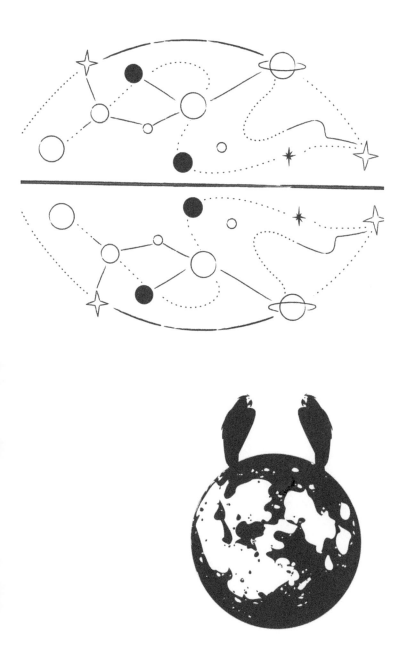

TREE

Your roots are dry
Your grass in dusty
Yet your air is incredible

LIVING MASTERPIECE

A living masterpiece is locked away deep within my chest and only you can unlock it

FLAME

Fire was in her eyes
Fury was in mine
Together, we started a flame

AROMATIC OCEAN

I can still smell you perfume across these oceans that separate us

123

DISASTER

*You are my natural disaster and yet there is
nothing natural about you*

MAGNETIC

Together, we are magnetic

STAR

You are among the stars
Chosen, you've been handpicked by the gods
Forever you will be my north star

STRENGTH

My strength comes from the fact that without you I am nothing but a man but with you, I am everything

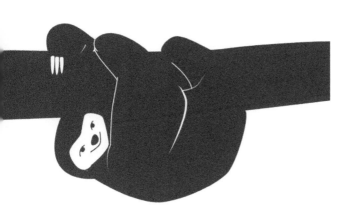

INVISIBLE

*If i was invisible and the only thing
visible was my heart, would you love me the
same*

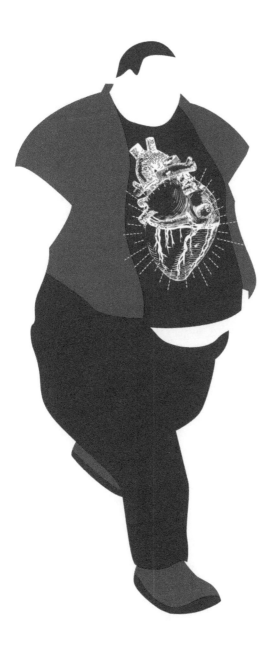

BOXED HEART

*In that box, there is everything you've always
asked of me and everything you've yet to see
so be careful my love because once you open
that box, you'll see all of me*

DOVES

She always wondered what was up there
So one day she flew away
with the doves that lived there

RIGHT

If I could, I would bring the moon and the sun
to you and cut my left lung

If I could, I would put them together like

a bun and serve to you, my dearest hun

But life is too short for all of that, and by that
time I'll be long overdone

And if you still want me to do all of that, then
you ain't the right one

THE MOON

Come fly with me to the moon
We can ascend like a balloon
Watch the sunset above the earth in the
afternoon
Feel what it feels like in early June
We can become immune
Because in the end
all I want is to stay up there with you,
on the moon

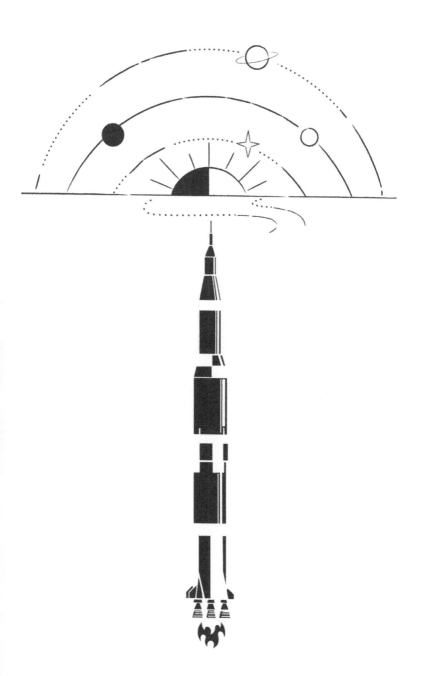

BLUE

There's a reason why the sky and
the oceans are red and that's
because your eyes are blue
All life resides in you
You are our blue

OURS

This is ours
This love and nobody can
take it from us

BEAUTIFUL

Beautiful are you, the one who looks in the mirror every morning despite your imperfections and brave are you, the one who smiles at such a site

YOU

All-day I can't help but think of you

Whenever I look at you, I no longer feel blue

My friends think I'm crazy, but that's just their cue

When I look at you chills run through my spine you have no clue

I always thought you were beautiful, your such view

My life has forever changed ever since you

stepped in and these words will never convey

how I feel about you

DESSERT

Deserted in this desert
I sit thinking of you
Eating my dessert

LAUGH-ATTACK

When was the last time you had
a laugh attack
When you nearly pissed your
pants because you found
something so amazingly quirky
and whack
A time when you couldn't breath
and felt like your chest
would crack
When total strangers looked at
you funny and themselves
smiled a crack

RUNNER

I ride
because i
chase the
wind
and the wind
chases me,
together we
run wild,
forever free

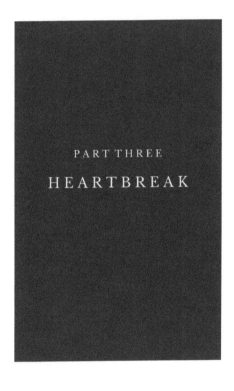

PART THREE

HEARTBREAK

Hearts are made to be broken

Oscar Wilde

LIMERENCE

They say love will find you, but over the years I have not been found

They say love will heal you, but I have not been bound
They say love will remunerate you, but I have not been crowned

The only thing I have is the river of tears in the palm of my hand

The only thing I hear is the buzzing of bees, oh they ache of my dreadful sound

Scuffling and tossing, I lay my head down
I reminisce of a day when my heart will be sound
When the thumping of my aching heart will finally be put down

But for the meantime, I will lay here awake on this ground
Waiting for my Ella to find me, unbound

I will have this piece of paradise called love, I will be abound

THUNDERSKY

There's a thunderstorm in my heart
A storm that rains blood and it's
lightning, blades
And every time the red sky
strikes a thunder bolt,
It tears me apart

SHARP SHARK

I swim in my own zone
Caged i find freedom
King i am dominance
Lonely is this aquarium
And watching are my
human masters

DEAF & DUMB & BLIND

Deaf are you when I mention my love
Dumb are you when I explain it
Blind are you when I show it

WINGS

Now i can't fly because you cut
and took my wings away

SWEET DREAMS

They float in my head when I go to bed

*Bouncing off strings into a distant land
deep into a space beyond my
consciousness*

*Yet when I awake, they buzz like a bee
aching for a drip of honey*

*Oh, how sweet it would be to taste my
dreams*

BALLOON

I am aimlessly climbing
On air like a balloon

WORLDS

How could life be so lonely in such a
interconnected world
How could two people sitting on the
same bench live in two different
worlds
Two realities driven by the
perspectives of their bipolar worlds
Only to be confused and left
spinning inside the same big
twirling world

TOYED HEART

Liar liar, she was a liar
She said she loved me so dire

That without me, life felt like hellfire

But standing here all alone I realize I am only a
flyer waiting to peek the interest of a buyer

Then to be placed down and left on a shelf to
expire

The misery each time leaves me dryer
I sing myself to sleep each night with a blue
choir

Hoping my Stella will one day come back into
my life and find me so that I may respire

I guess today is not that day so i'll have to wait
until tomorrow to inquire

PANTHER

Like a panther you hide
feasting in the dark
over my dead heart

BROKEN

You were meant to help me when I bled
howl with me when I plead
hung with me in my time of need
but never to abandon me because of
your jealously or greed

BITTER

I expected the best
Received the worst
It was aN exceptional delusion

EXPENSIVE

I was only a clown and you were a
volunteer in my circus
You gave me your heart and
trying to impress you i dropped it like glass on
hard pavement
You paid the price and for that i can never
forgive myself
Because now you are broken and
there is no other heart
that could ever replace yours

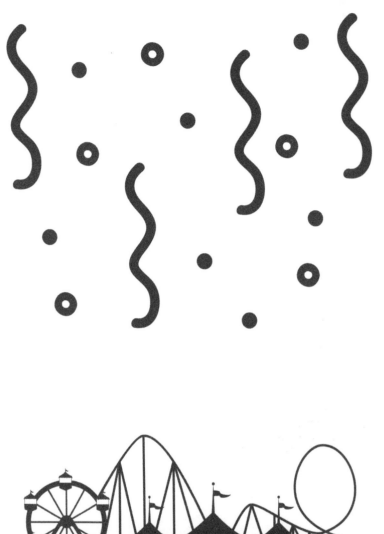

ALLIGATOR

Admiring my own beauty through the
reflecting mirror of the clear, salty, lake,
you jumped out of it, jealous and ugly as an
alligator and bit my head off

DISMISSED

*You dismissed me when i needed you most, now
i'll dismiss you becuase i need you the least*

BONES

Broken bones
Shattered heart
Bruised eyes
Busted lip,
When will I learn to let go and let this
relationship zip?

COBRA

At times i feel as if i sleep with a beast
a delicate cobra that wraps me tightly
and tells me in my ear,
everything is going to be okay;
eventually to end up strangling me

DEMONS

My demons drink with me
My angels pray for me
My parents cry for me
My friends laugh at me
My lover threatens me
Oh well, I guess I'll drink to another with my
mini enemies

TINY DANCER

Soon you will run out of moves
The music will stop playing
And i'll stop watching.
What will you tell me then?

APOLOGY

An apology is meant from the heart not from the mind

THUMPING

Thumping
Pumping
It broke
What,
My heart

STRANGER

She is a stranger
With a strange face
I once knew

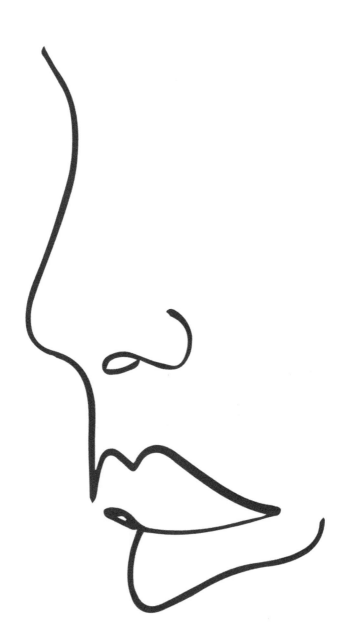

193

RIVER TEARS

A river of tears sit on the edge of
my eyes every time i think of you

TIME TRAVELLING

*At times i wish i could travel
back into the past so we could
meet again*

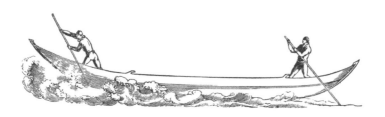

LOSSED LOVE

You agree you'd never fight for
something you don't
love
yet you fight with someone you don't
love
fighting for something that will never
love you
back

TOGETHER

*Maybe I'll meet someone who is broken like me
and maybe we can put each other back
together and become, we*

HONEY BEE

*What happened to chasing each
other around the kitchen,
pretending i was your bee
and you were my honey*

MYSTERY

You were a puff of smoke and like a child
I walked Into you with arms full of embrace

DIZZY

*Dizzy in the dizzying spin of my
loneliness*

*I spin down a twirl towards a
lowliness*

*Deep into the darkness of my
horrifying mental unwellness*

Hunted by the thoughts that whisper

*Your life is meaningless, so why
 don't you just end all of this!*

207

MOCKINGBIRD

A whistle, a bird, a bird whistled

Drip, drip, drip, it drizzled

Then and only then, rang the sound of a pistol

Silence. A bird fell like a missile

Laying there a hunter tickled, a mockingbird as

It sucked its final whistle

Then picked up by its feet, washed, and kindled

The End.

Thanks for reading!

Lightning Source UK Ltd.
Milton Keynes UK
UKHW051906081119
353090UK00011B/163/P